Acknowledgments

There are many people who have taught me so much in my professional and personal life. Although I can't thank you all individually, please know that I never forget about you.

have done for me.

To all of you who gave me a chance, to those who took a risk on me when I needed work, who took chances on me early with a new web company, and those who stayed with us throughout 16 years, I am forever grateful. It wouldn't have been possible without your trust.

Mom, I've known for many years all the hard decisions and sacrifices you made during my time on this planet. You are my mom and I am deeply grateful. I have learned a lot from you about resilience.

Milton Hershey - Although I never had the privilege of meeting you in person you have made a huge impact on my life. Your generous gift of Milton Hershey School would not have changed my life. Although it is true that I have done the work, it was actually you who gave me the chance to do it. It was also you who instilled the values Milton Hershey School still lives by today and continues using to influence the lives of more than 10,000 children.

Dan Candell – Dan, my podcast co-host, is a true friend. It's an honor to have you in mine and I know I can reach you at any hour. Your ideas are innovative, your support unwavering, your friendship is incomparable!

Jeff Cobb, Sonja STetzler, Gary Wilbers, - You have been my sounding board. You supported me when I was unsure where to take this book.

Erik Wahl - Although 2011 seems like a long time ago, to me it feels like yesterday. I learned a lot from you that day in Leominster Massachusetts about creativity, thinking outside of the box and trying new things. This was also the day that set me on my path to becoming a speaker. It's an honor to have you mentor me and provide insight into the industry. It's an honor to be #ArtDropSniper. I am grateful for everything I have learned from your company.

Erica Milano: A simple conversation of five minutes on a Pop Warner field, 2001, changed my life forever! Your words and encouragement will be etched in my heart forever. This conversation was the seed for a successful website agency that I later sold. We are grateful!

Foreword

Think back to the time someone sent you a present in the mail or simply reached out to let you know they care. It makes you feel good, doesn't it? Think about it.

Think back to the time you were approached by someone and knew that it was because they needed something. It is a human need for love, care and recognition. But, the connections we make with others must be real.

Matt Ward is able to ensure that his generosity, loyalty, and giving nature are always genuine and altruistic. It was initially hard to believe that Matt Ward's generosity, loyalty, and giving nature is just his nature. I didn't know if it was his personality or one his core values. After Matt's presentation, I was amazed at how he transformed dozens upon dozens of business owners into caring individuals. They were all instilled the same values and principles that have made Matt and every other business he owned successful. It's an art, a skill, and a trait that genuinely cares for others.

Matt Ward was the first person I met at a local BNI. His larger-than-life personality was intriguing. As I attended more meetings, I began to study Matt (that's my job, study human behavior) and noticed his amazing ability to make everyone feel valued. Matt discovered that I was having problems with my new laptop computer. After the meeting, he offered to meet me for breakfast and teach me how to use the new laptop. He had the exact same one. After many more interactions, we began to work together on several projects. He did have to bend my arm, I'm sorry. After many failed business relationships with others, I resolved to never again work with anyone unless we could both contribute equally.

We developed a program for golf instruction that we sold to pros. It was moderately profitable. Matt contacted me after taking a break. Matt called me one night late at night and said, "Dan! You have a great voice on the radio." Do you think about being on the radio? My ego got in my way so I replied, "Matt! You all know that I've been on the radio ..." He introduced me to the idea of starting a joint venture podcast. Although it was difficult to get started, the podcast has been a huge success, almost two years later and nearly 100 episodes later!

You might be asking yourself, "Why is this important?" Through sharing this podcast platform and attending many events with Matt, I realized something: He has a unique way to care for people. He listens, observes, and then acts. This is what's so amazing. He doesn't expect anything in return. It does it benefit him and his business ventures. Absolutely! It is his attitude towards his giving nature that is most remarkable.

This was a trait I thought was only Matt's personality. I began to question him about his caring values and he changed my mind. It was amazing to see him instill these same values and principles in me and others who have had the privilege of hearing him speak or are part of one of his programs. Matt's book is proof of that.

Although it sounds absurd that people need to be taught the values of generosity and caring, it is true. These values are slowly disappearing among individuals and businesses.

Matt has a great program called CarePackage that he will show you how to implement. These principles can be applied to your business and life to make lifelong connections, customers, and referral sources through the art and science of caring. It is indeed an art that can be easily taught and applied in your life and business.

This book's content was simple and effective, which I found amazing after being shown. Here is a quick example of CarePackage's power in action. A group of 130 sales professionals listened to me speak in Las Vegas. I was the closing keynote, and the last speaker. I decided to stay to watch the closing ceremony after my presentation. The organizer of the event asked everyone to speak up and state how they would implement the information they had gained over the weekend. The entire room began to chant "I CAN, and I WILL!" after each individual had given an action item. I didn't realize it at the time but this became the group's mantra. I quickly wrote down the words "I can, I will" in my notebook. The co-organizer asked me, "Hello Dan, I love your notebook. Where did you get it?" I laughed and replied, "On Amazon!"

After I left, I wrote down the names of the key people in the organization, Sarah, and Jim. Next to Sarah's names, I wrote the words "I can, & I will". Next to Jims's name I wrote "productivity journal." Then I flew home and continued my business.

Three weeks later, as I was strolling through a local department shop, I noticed a section with wooden signs bearing sayings. One of them jumped out at my face when I stopped. I said, "Well I'll be damned ..." The sign had the words "I can, and will" written across it. It cost $4.99. It was only $4.99. I grabbed it immediately and added it to my cart. This reminded me of Jim's comment about how much he liked my journal. So I ordered the journal on my phone, and it was shipped to Jim with a small note. When I got back home, I packed the sign and sent it to Sarah.

It was exciting. I was even more excited to see their replies... I was disappointed after a few weeks of not hearing back. Matt called me and I said "DUDE!" I did my thing, I cared! They didn't care about me back, but what the hell? Matt reminded us that CarePackage is not for them. It's a way to make people feel good and it makes us feel good. We do not do it to receive a reply from them. It's because we care." This was a huge realization for me. It's true.

I received a thank you note from Jim and Sarah a few weeks later. Although I don't know what will happen, I know it was a small gesture of kindness that brought smiles to the faces of both Sarah and Jim. It is very simple.

Are there other things? Absolutely. Matt will be sharing his secrets, formula, and special art to help you get more customers and referrals through CarePackage. This system is one that anyone can and should use. You can be sure that even if your values are already similar, you will still find more ways to make them stronger.

I am grateful for the opportunity to share my experiences with all of you. It is an honor to know that this art will be used by more people in their networks. Be well, do your best, and stay true to yourself.

Introduction to CarePackage

Ronii Bartles introduced me to me in 2009 through a mutual friend. Ronii Bartles is a West Virginia woman who lives in Charleston, South Carolina. She loves every moment of it. She is a marketer and has a great eye for design. Ronii is meticulously organized and executes all marketing projects she undertakes flawlessly. She is an excellent communicator, a good listener, and a passionate wine drinker. Ronii is a focused, independent, and driven entrepreneur who can kick butt and take on names. She enjoys writing content both for clients and herself. She loves storytelling and putting in a few one-liners. That is why I enjoy reading her marketing blogs.

She creates amazing content that is enjoyed by everyone, including me. This helped me to get to know Ronii, both what she was like 10 and now who she is. I discovered what Ronii enjoyed most: her work, her hobbies and other important things. These lessons are sprinkled throughout her writings. She finds a way for her to be authentic in her writing. Sometimes, she puts herself fully into her blogs. Sometimes she sprinkles bits of gold and nuggets with detail on her blog.

A lightbulb erupted as I was reading her blog in my office. The lightbulb illuminated her article like an old lamppost on a dark country road. Although I don't know the exact content of her blog, I will always remember one morsel she added to that article. One line in her blog proclaimed her love for chocolate-covered bacon. What? Yes! Yes! I immediately assigned an employee to hunt down chocolate-covered bacon. After a while, it was finally done. We shipped the gift to Ronii in South Carolina.

It arrived within hours and her social media pages lit up like a Christmas tree. Ronii shared photos, stories and details about the chocolate-covered bacon and my web agency inConcertWeb Solutions. It wasn't exactly what I expected, but I'll take it!

Now, I am astonished that she was so enthusiastic about sharing her story.

Social media. She was an expert marketer. I should have known that she would share the story online immediately.

The series of actions that led to the social media posts was something that I thought about for weeks. CarePackage was born from those days of thinking. It took me many years to establish the framework and achieve the business results.

You don't need to be Ronii. To share positive messages on social media, you don't need to be a marketer. You'll see more people sharing their love on social media. This is just one way to build stronger connections and closer bonds with your contacts.

Ronii was a constant source of referrals to my website agency over many years. Even after the sale of inConcert in 2018, she still refers business. Why is she referring? Is it because of chocolate-covered bacon It's unlikely. It might, however, be part of it.

The Premise

It is well-known that people only do business with those they trust, like and respect. It's much more than that, I believe. People want to do business only with people they trust, like, and respect. Ronii was interested in referring us. She wanted a reliable source who would deliver on their promises, on time and within budget. That was what we did consistently. However, she needed someone to call her back. This seems to be a common problem in the online world. We were able to provide a reliable and responsive service that people could access. In fact, 65% if our new clients said that they couldn't reach their current provider.

In the 16 years I was the owner of the web agency, I have always sought out the best way to do things. I was focused on automation and optimization. But I kept returning to what really matters, one-to-one communication among trusted contacts. Our website agency found many ways to make sure we were always in the forefront of our contacts' minds.

When speaking to business owners about advertising and marketing, I ask them: "With a show hand, how many of your opinion word of mouth is the best way to get new business?" The overwhelming answer is more than 90%. I then ask: "How many of your processes have you found to increase word of mouth referrals?" The results are disconcerting. It was always lower than 10 percent.

We know that word of mouth referrals are the best way to get clients. So why don't we work every day to increase our referrals? It's okay, sometimes life gets in the way. But we always find new shiny objects. This happened to me too. In the four years I was in charge of my agency, almost 75 percent of new clients came from our partners. They were constantly referring us. The remaining 25% was split between clients and other sources. The remaining 25% was split into two categories: clients (20%) and other (5%) Other included sources we didn't know about and Google search results. Advertising didn't result in any new clients for our websites!

These numbers were meticulously tracked. We not only asked our clients how they found us when we onboarded them, but also noted this information in our CRM (Customer Relations Management) Software as well as in their file. This matrix was a key part of our obsession. This is why you should also be obsessed with it. It's a repeatable system that allows for more word-of-mouth referrals. To increase your referrals, you must know who to communicate with.

Rule Number One: Stay in Touch

No matter how much you may be bothering someone else, if they don't keep in touch with you, you won't get any referrals. You will receive more referrals if you can find new ways to reach your contacts. It's as simple as that. Businesses advertise and market because they want to be remembered when someone searches for their services. It is important to keep in touch with people. This will make you more visible and allows you to get more referrals.

Personal CarePackage

You must think of creative ways to reach your contacts in order to cut through the marketing noise that bombards them every day. The key is to create your personal care package. It is a collection of actions you take to make sure you are always top of mind for your contacts. Each contact will have a different approach, but it won't be drastically different. You might send a chocolate-covered bacon to your contact. Or a customized bag of trail mix to your contact. To ensure that you send the right item to your contact, it is important to understand their preferences.

This is your personal CarePackage. You may have been blessed enough to be given a care package by someone you love. The recipient is the focus of care packages. This is the purpose of the whole process. It's all about the recipient and not you.

The Four Pillars of CarePackage

Before I get into the four pillars it is important to understand that you are sending care packages because your contact cares. It won't work if you do this to obtain a referral. You'll regret it. Your contacts will quickly see through your lack of genuine care and concern for them.

Joey Coleman, my friend and author, wrote that the best gifts are meaningful and personal. They show a level of care that is appropriate for the relationship. They can also be gifts of time. These are personal phone calls or emails. Your time and effort are gifts that you give to your contact. Referrals by word of mouth are a result of caring for others. They will care for you, and your business.

Pillar 1 – Over-delivery

Over-delivery is inherent in transactions of any kind. Transactions usually involve money, but they don't always have to. This is especially true if you volunteer. You must find ways to exceed your client's expectations. You over-deliver because you care about your clients and the results they get from your services. Because you care and the fact that you have over-deliver is obvious to your client, they will be more inclined to refer you to other people they know.

This question is often asked of me when it comes to over-delivery. "Should your under-promise be met with over-delivery?" The simple answer is no. If you make under-promises, it is because you want to over-deliver. This is dishonest.

Pillar 2 - Listening

Listening is defined as listening. It refers to the ability to hear. The Merriam-Webster dictionary describes listening in three different ways:

- "to pay attention to sound"
- "To hear something with thoughtful attention: Give consideration"
- "to be alert to catch an expected sound"

All these definitions refer to sound or hearing. However, you can listen with your eyes as well. What if the Merriam Webster definitions of sound and hearing were replaced with visual terms? These are the results:

- "to pay attention to ~~sound~~"
- "To hear something with thoughtful attention: Give consideration"
- "to be alert to catch ~~an~~ "something" expected ~~sound~~"

Think about how the world might look if everyone in your network was willing to share information that could be very useful to you in future interactions.

Pillar 3 - Surprise

It is powerful to surprise someone by your actions. Comedy comedians often use surprise in their jokes. The comedians give context and then throw in the punchline, which is often not what you expected. Comedy comedians are funny because their punchlines are often unexpected.

You order something from Amazon, and it comes in 2 days with Prime shipping. When the package arrives at your door, you are unlikely to feel butterflies. The next day, an unexpected package arrives at your door. To find out who sent it, you immediately look at the return address. Your pulse quickens. This was sent by who? What is in the box? You have not even opened the box, but the sender has made an impressive impression. It's a powerful way for people to connect, no matter who they are.

Pillar 4 – Non-self-serving Acts

Your actions should serve your contact and not yourself. Let's take, for example, the case where you love chocolate but your contact is allergic. Imagine what it would do if you sent your contact chocolate. You would be eager to experience the surprise. I was curious who sent me the package. What could it possibly have been? Then your contact would open the package to find that it was chocolate. Your good intentions would not last.

It is a self-serving act that I often see: people sending thank you cards with a business card. The card should be about the recipient only when you send a thank-you card. If you include a business card with your thank you card, it turns that experience into something personal. It's not a gift of time or effort nor a card. It's a way to send your business card through the post and it's self-serving.

You can remove your marketing materials and yourself from the mix to create an act of selflessness that is key to your personal CarePackage!

Combining Pillars

These pillars should not be taken from the book and put to use.

alone. These can often be combined to create meaningful interactions and experiences with your contact. Let's take a look at Ronii's chocolate-covered bacon again. In this case, I listened with all my ears, I heard her words, and then I surprised myself. This was not self-serving. I did not ask for anything in return and didn't share any information on social media that indicated that I had sent the gift. To make it happen, I used three of the four pillars.

I often find that the clients I work with don't seek out the pillar they should use or work within. They take action with their contacts, and then reflect on the action and the pillar(s). It is a great way of continuing to evaluate how well you care for your contacts by reflecting on what you did after taking action.

This book features the strategies that I have used over time. I hope you will find this book useful in connecting with your contacts.

Birthdays Beyond Facebook: Birthday Card Revival

Let's face it. Every birthday is special, no matter how many you have celebrated. People remember your birthday and you will never forget it. Facebook makes it easy to celebrate birthdays. All you need is a few clicks. Some people might even post a celebratory image. When we see 200 birthday messages posted to our Facebook wall, we feel a sense of recognition. The rush is temporary, and while it gives us an immediate boost, it's fleeting. We know 200 people chose the path of least resistance.

Let's instead find a way to be more real with our birthday friends. Let's not forget the old ways of connecting with our friends around birthdays. A stack of thoughtful, funny, and clever birthday cards can be kept on your desk. You can then choose the best one for your contact and address it with a personal note. Finally, you can mail it. This is where the note comes in. It should be short and personal, but relevant to past conversations. It is a great way to express your gratitude and show that you care about your contact. It's a wonderful thing to get a personal card in the midst of all the junk mail and bills. Your special touch will be remembered by your contact forever.

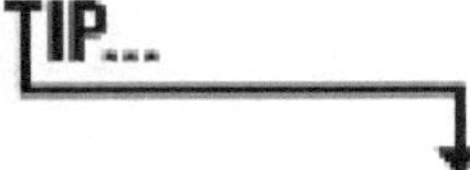

It's simple to find out the birthday of your contact if you don't have it. Although many people will list their birthdays without including the year, it's not necessary when you send a thoughtful birthday message.

Java Jumpstart

What could be better than a quick cup of coffee in the middle a busy, deadline-driven work day? When you least expect it, a freshly-brewed cup of hot coffee delivered right to your door. It's certain that surprise java boosts will brighten the day of your contact. Quickly say hello to your contact after you have finished the coffee and mention that you appreciate their time. Respect their time when doing this.

You can ask your contact how they drink their coffee. If that is the case, you can opt for black with cream and sugar. You can leave the rest of the doctoring to them. Drop by to ask your special delivery driver how they drink their coffee. Make a note in the notes section on your phone's contact record.

Next time, bring your favorite caffe latte.

Don't overstay your welcome. If your contact does not invite you to stay, do not spend more than five minutes in their office. Keep it brief and sweet. It is important that they remember the surprise coffee and not your interruptions of their daily tasks.

We are grateful for your business

Keep a stack of thank-you cards on your desk. You never know who you might be able to help.

When you need it. It's one of the easiest ways to show your appreciation for your contacts. Send a thank-you note to your contacts when they decide to do business with us.

We often get caught up in chasing new sales, and then we move on to the next one. Give your contact a moment of gratitude. Although we are always grateful for the business, it is not always easy to express our gratitude in a way that our contacts notice. These people are what keep you in business.

Here's an example of a Thank You Note I sent:

Hello Lisa,

I am grateful for the opportunity to speak at your conference. It was a pleasure and a great honor to be invited. The conference was energetic and the audience was very open to ideas. It was a wonderful experience.

Keep in touch. If I can be of any assistance, please let me know.

With gratitude,

Matt

You can take five to ten minutes to create a thank you note for your business that you can use as an example. When it comes time to thank someone specific, personalize the note. Your contact will feel special when you add the finishing touches.

Swagalicious

You might not be aware that SWAG stands for Stuff We All Get. Y The thing about swag, however, is that not everyone has access to the same items. You might have some swag your contacts would love. It's easy to have swag at your office. Get to know your contacts and choose the right swag for them. Then package it up and send it off. They will be delighted.

You'll be more than happy to give away swag. If you're at an expo or trade show and know someone who is obsessed with highlighters, you can keep your eyes open for vendors giving them away. You can make a lot of contacts by making the rounds. You can then put together a small collection of highlighters from the trade shows and send it to your contact. You'll be remembered fondly by them, as they will remember you fondly for all their highlighter-related adventures.

My friend worked as a radio DJ, and had access to the best swag. I was envious of her swag! She got tickets to Six Flags, Six Flags ski lift tickets, movie tickets, concert tickets, festival tickets, t-shirts from various brands and branded apparel from the radio station. She would always stop by the office of a contact to give them one of these amazing giveaways whenever she received something. It was a hit. It was a great gift. Even if the gift is swag, everyone loves to receive gifts. Bonus points if you don't brand the swag that you give away.

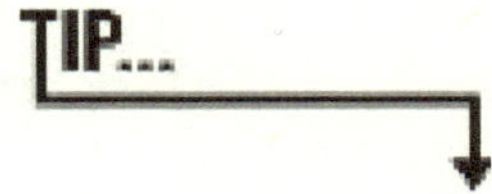

You could become a swag-scoring machine. You can find cool swag at races, festivals, art shows, sporting events, and races. It's possible to find the perfect gift for someone you know and make their day.

R.E.S.P.E.C.T.

ho doesn't love to receive positive feedback? The old saying is that people will not remember what you say, but how you made them feel. People sometimes forget to express their positive thoughts to their family and friends in this fast-paced world. People often lose touch in a technological world. This can be a great opportunity to stand out and make your mark in the market.

Spend some time identifying the strengths of your contacts and the characteristics, habits, and traits that you most respect. Next, choose the most effective way to show your respect for them. You can tailor your approach to each person. Your feelings can be shared in person, by phone with a card or email. Email is my last choice. It's less personal and can get lost amongst the flood of emails that your contact receives.

These are some things you should look out for in contacts that you may respect:

- Hustle and Drive
- Commitment
- Positive attitude
- Financial acumen
- Daily habits
- Morning routine
- Sense of calm
- Time management
- Leadership
- Articulate

Thoughtfulness

TIP...

If you are sharing what you admire about your contact, be sure to add a specific example of the trait, habit, or quality. They will see that you are paying attention and truly mean what they say.

#NewsWorthySharing

We live in an age of social media overload. There are photos of foodie meals, W photos about silly pets tricks and selfies galore.

Oui! Oui! Holding up the Leaning Tower of Pisa. It won't fall! The dictum of the time is "I share, therefore I am." Let's face the facts: Some things are more shareable than others, such as your contacts' major news. Here's some news that will stop you from clicking the "share" button.

Maybe your contact is hosting a holiday sale or celebrating a ribbon cutting. Perhaps they are launching a new product or service or a new website. Tag your contact on social media and share newsworthy updates about their business. Tag your contact to let them know you shared their news. It shows that you care about your contact's business and the content they share. They want the word to spread if they have posted it. Make sure to use social media to spread the word and amplify their news! The more the merrier!

TIP...

Tags are used to identify someone in a status update, photo, or post that you share. Use @Contact's name if you use Facebook, Instagram, Twitter.

Take the time to give thanks

You can't thank enough people for their attention and time.

Y, whether you are in person, or by other means like email, text, or cards. It is worth taking a moment to show gratitude.

Keep a large number of thank-you cards handy so you are prepared for every occasion. Write a thank-you note after you have met with the contact. You don't need to write a lengthy letter. A short note suffices. Thank you for meeting with me. Also, mention some of the topics you discussed. It should be personal. Avoid using generic content as it will reduce the card's impact. This card is not about speeding up your time. It's about strengthening and deepening your relationships.

Here's a recent example:

Hi John,

It was a pleasure to have you take the time out of your busy schedule to meet with me. It was a pleasure to learn more about you and your business' core values and hear your Taco Tuesday story. Your daughter's basketball team will win the tournament! We look forward to seeing each other again.

Be well,
Matt

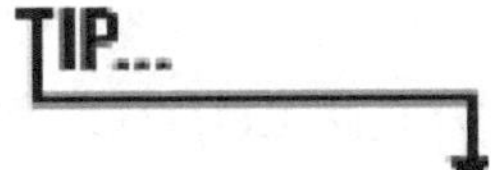

Take five to ten minutes after your phone or face-to-face meeting to write a thank you note. This will make your conversation fresh and allow you to add more personal details that will make a bigger impact.

Brighten Someone's Day

There is almost nothing more satisfying than being praised with a sincere compliment. This makes the person being complimented feel good and brightens their day. What are some things you should compliment your contacts? You can compliment your contacts on their professional achievements, awards, milestones, or anniversaries. Your contact might have won a crucial meeting, launched a product, landed a contract or run a successful event. You can see what your contacts are posting on social media and how they feel about their achievements. This information may help you to give a compliment to your contact. You will make their day.

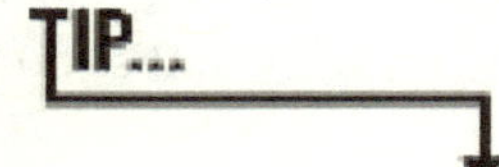

Keep your compliments business-related. Don't make your contacts uncomfortable by your compliments.

Be Known as a Connector

Each of us has a wealth of connections. Each of us has E networks that can help propel our contacts to new heights.

The missing ingredient is a way to connect people. LinkedIn is a great tool, but it lacks a personal touch. This is where you come in.

One of your contacts may be interested in meeting someone you know. Make that introduction. Your contact and the third party will benefit from the connection. Connectors are able to build lasting and satisfying relationships. You will be highly sought after by people who discover that they can turn to you for help in connecting with others and finding the resources they need.

Keven, a friend, sent me a text asking me if I knew anyone who could install and equip video conferencing software in his company's conference rooms. Keven knew that I had the connections to help him get what he wanted. I reached out and connected him to the right person through my network. This is something that happens a lot to me because I am transparent with everyone about my strong network and proactive connections. It's a gift that keeps giving, and you'll be happy to hear that building networks can be a joy.

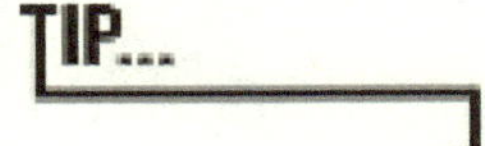

Do not wait for someone to contact you to make a connection. Make introductions and connect with others. It's possible that the next connection will change someone's entire life. Your contact will be forever grateful.

Knowledge is Power

Anyone can believe that knowledge is power. In the digital age, knowledge is power. Consider the software, apps, or tools you are skilled in and how they might be of benefit to your contacts. You may think you know everything about your contacts, but you never know what shared knowledge could do for them. Nothing is better than sharing your knowledge with someone you already know. Reach out to them and gauge their interest. If they are interested, you can agree to train them and schedule a time. It will show that you care about your contact and how they succeed.

Offer to teach your contact a tool via a virtual session. This can be done if they live in another city. It's like being there.

Make a Splash with a Personalized Gift

If you think back to the most meaningful gifts that you have ever received, you will likely recall the ones that took into consideration your passions and interests. They were personalized for you. A personalized gift has more intrinsic value that a generic one. If you are thinking of gifting a person a gift, think about what they would appreciate. Your gift should be thoughtful. How can you get the information you need to personalize your gift without giving away the surprise? Here's how it happened.

I was going to an event and wanted to tell the host how much the content had helped me. I had read his book, and listened to all his podcasts, even those where he was a guest. I wanted to thank you in a special way.

Based on his stories, I was able to connect the dots. I knew that he owned a boat, and that his friends loved to drink wine on the boat. I had an idea to give him a personalized gift with his boat's name. Because I wanted to surprise him, I decided not to ask him directly. Through internet research, I found his boat's name as well as the logo. I ordered a wooden wine opener set that had his name engraved on it. He loved it! It was very affordable at $30, and made quite the splash.

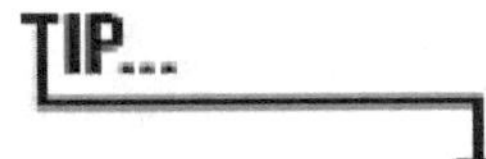

Through emails, conversations, and social media posts, you can find out what is important to your contact.

Boost Your Contacts' Industry Knowledge

Even if your contacts are aware of the benefits of learning about their industries,

They rarely have the time or patience to learn new things and become better businesspeople. Why? They're too busy delivering products and services to customers. How can you solve this problem? Do your research!

You will be able to keep your contacts informed by sharing cutting-edge articles and resources. Each week, send an article to a new contact. This should be done at a particular time each week. Spend no more than 10 minutes looking through articles in order to find the perfect one for your contact. This will allow you to add one or two more contacts to increase your reach!

A simple note in your email should explain why the resource or article is useful to you. This is key to resource sharing. You can decide how many articles you want to send. You should remember that too many articles in one email can make your contact feel overwhelmed. It won't work. They will simply glance at the email and not read the article, so the resource sharing won't be effective.

This has been a habit that I have maintained over the years, and it is always a great compliment from my contacts. They were clearly grateful that I went above-and-beyond for them.

TIP...

Create a Google Alert. Google will search for keywords that are relevant to the industry of your contact and send you an email. Emails related to the alert keyword will be sent to you. Send your contact the article link by clicking here.

Genie in a Bottle

Who doesn't wish to have a genie in the bottle that can answer all of their questions W and grant their every wish? You are correct! There is a genie that will respond immediately to your queries. It's called Google. It can't grant every wish yet, but it's working on it! For those who gathered information the old school way-- using libraries and encyclopedias--Google is nothing short of miraculous.

Google does more than just respond to queries about how to set up QuickBooks or how to make a viral video. It can also help build relationships with contacts. This is a great idea if you want to let your contact know that you care about them. Google the industry of your contact or something relevant to their business. Find websites that inspire and spark passion in your contact. Sites that have the potential to positively affect their product, service, or bottom line. To find the most valuable websites, you must carefully vet them.

Once you have identified a few websites, send an email with the links and a note explaining how the websites can benefit your contact's company. Your initiative will impress your contact and make them feel like you are going the extra mile. Your contact will remember you as a reliable resource for any questions or concerns they may have. A little bit of legwork can make a big difference in today's busy world.

TIP...

There is a genie that will respond immediately to your queries. The Googling Genie will amaze your contacts and keep you at the top of their minds.

→

Don't Worry.

Curiosity Never Killed the Cat

Contrary to popular belief, curiosity doesn't kill the cat. It won't kill you. You will find that curiosity about the life of your contact can open doors that you didn't know existed.

Let's suppose you meet at your contact's workplace and notice photos of her family jumping bungee. It almost looks like they are in New Zealand or Australia. This is why you might think so. In the collage, she is seen posing with a Kangaroo. Your contact tells you about the photo collage. It was a trip she had always wanted to take. Her family was harrowed by a crocodile incident, but they survived. It's called "The Croc almost Ate My Husband" by her. You both will be in stitches.

You admire the abstract art on the wall opposite and ask the artist. She proudly declares it hers, but she pauses. You claim that it was made by someone famous, and she is clearly humbled by your compliments.

You've created a lasting connection with your contact by taking the time to observe her world and asking about her life. You didn't notice to sell anything or ask for things in a selfish manner. To build trust and strengthen your relationship with your contact, you took notice. People enjoy talking about their lives, their hobbies and their families. They will remember you as someone they trust and who is authentic when they have the opportunity.

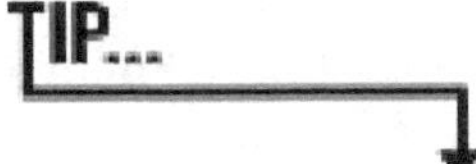

You will find new opportunities by being curious about the lives of your contacts. Use the rule of three to ask three related questions. This will allow you to dig deeper into the topic.

Read All About It!

If your contact appears in the newspaper, or in a magazine article about them, grab the I link from the article and send it in to a local awards organization to receive a plaque. People are not always featured in the news.

It shows you care and are attentive to your contact.

It has always resulted in a hug when I do this for others. Even though that is not the ultimate goal, people are still amazed that you took the time to make a memento. This gift is perceived to be far more valuable than its actual cost.

This was for Jack, an employee in a new IT company. He posted a Facebook article from the local business magazine about an award his company received. Although I don't have the whole story, Jack is featured in the photo. He poses in front of the sign and not the owner. This intrigued me and I wanted to ensure Jack had a copy of the article. I made a plaque to capture the moment. Jack even gave me a hug, in case anyone was wondering!

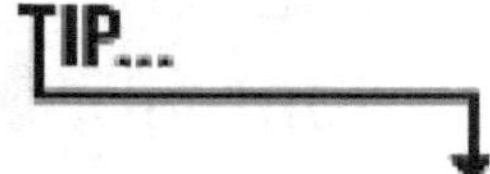

Personalize the plaque for the individual when you place your order. A classic wooden plaque is best for traditional contacts. For someone who is fashion-forward, choose a contemporary style.

Tap Your Contacts' Expertise

Helping others grow professionally and personally is part of H's mission. We can all learn from each other and share our experiences. Sharing our expertise is a great way to help others achieve their goals. You can ask your friends for business advice in the spirit of goodwill. It depends on the relationship, though I would recommend that business topics be kept to a minimum. You will decide if it is appropriate to discuss personal topics.

Asking for advice builds trust with your contacts. Reaching out to other business owners for advice is a great way to grow your business and show that you value their business acumen. You will be grateful for their knowledge.

Masterminds are groups made up of like-minded colleagues that meet regularly to brainstorm solutions and help each other. You might consider creating or seeking out a mastermind. This will allow you to surround yourself with people you trust and who you can reach quickly.

——————————→

Is Anybody Listening?

Have you noticed how everyone seems to be competing for airtime in this noisy age? It doesn't matter if it's a meeting or after-work get-together; people seem to have lost touch with communication. Is anyone really listening when there are so many people talking?

You may have a memory of a time when someone shared something important with you and brought it up later. Maybe it was something positive, such as a promotion or a stressful event like a presentation to your company's board of directors. What did that make you feel? It was likely that you felt that your colleague remembered something you shared with them. This colleague probably holds a special place within your heart.

Communication is a two-way process. If no one is listening, is communication really happening? It is a rare skill to be able to listen and not just hear, but it is a skill that can be learned. Your personal care package should include listening.

Perhaps your contact mentioned that they were going to a meeting or that their child's team reached the finals of the baseball league. Spend a few minutes of your day to reach out to your contact about the meeting or the game. Your contact will not only be thrilled to share the outcome, but they will also be impressed that you cared enough to reach back out. These simple touches are often forgotten in today's digital age. This makes them even more memorable.

TIP...

You can also make a note of what your contact said and jot it down so you can recall later. It's okay to have little reminders to keep in touch with your contacts.

A Little Help Goes A Long Way

When was the last time you were offered help by someone without strings attached? If you are like most people, chances are that there isn't many offers of help from family and friends. It's not because people don't care, but that we are often too busy with our own responsibilities. They might all fall if we added one more thing to the juggling game!

Even though you are probably very busy, I suggest that you check in with your contacts regularly and ask how you can help. Do not panic, but ask your contacts if they can help you. Hear me. You don't have to offer to help someone with major projects, such as moving. It's a great way for check-in conversations to begin by reaching out to your contact and asking "What can you do to help?" It's a simple offer of your time to help someone. Even if they decline, this offer is very meaningful. It is important that they know you are trying to help.

TIP...

Be authentic. Don't be too salesy. Otherwise, you will come across as one who is trying to sell. Be open to helping others in this conversation.

Lights, Camera, Action!

Have you ever wanted to direct, produce and act in your very own video? Facebook Live makes it possible. It's difficult to make something unique with so many competitors for attention on smartphones, tablets and laptops. Videos are more popular than text or still graphics.

Create a quick Facebook Live video next time you're with a contact. The video can be set up as a business conversation featuring the contact's company. This will give your contact free exposure. Your contact will appreciate your willingness to share their content even if they aren't your ideal audience.

What exactly is a Facebook Live Video? A Facebook Live video is a live post that you make on Facebook. You'll be able to see live viewers and the real-time stream comments during your broadcast. The broadcast will remain on your page's timeline until it ends.

You can make a live video about them!

1. Set a goal. Know your goals for the live video.
2. Be the interviewer. Ask questions about your guest and their business.

3. Pay attention to what they say and then ask relevant follow-up questions.

A Video Co-Star is Born

In recent years, ideos have gained popularity on social media. These ideos are more popular than images or photos and more likely to be retweeted by Twitter. If you are interested in joining the video revolution, it's time.

haven't already.

Ask your contacts if they'd like to appear in a video about business that you post on Facebook, Instagram or Twitter. You share the spotlight with your contacts when you include them. While most people will accept your invitation, some may not be open to the idea because they are too shy to take photos. It's okay! No problem! Your invitation just shows that you care about them.

If your contact is open to the idea, they may ask questions about the video's content, purpose, and why you invited it. Before inviting your star, it is important to consider these questions. You will be prepared if you know your purpose in advance. This video is used by most clients who I work with to present their business contacts in short interviews lasting no more than three minutes. After the business is done, have fun with it. You will get more attention if your business is lively. It might even go viral!

TIP...

After you have shot the video, upload it on social media. Tag all people in the video as well as anyone you think might be interested in seeing the video. Include a call-to-action in your post. This could include contact information for your contact or a plug for their product or service. This video could make a great promotional tool for both you and your contact.

Cutting Through the Noise

How did we become so busy it was dizzying? Our inboxes are overflowing with requests, questions, and tasks. No matter the task, the deadline is ASAP. Some people have developed allergies to their email inboxes. What's the best way for you to cut through all the noise?

Texting is a great way to cut through all the noise, since most people are constantly on their phones. It's not easy to tell who texts and who doesn't from your contacts. Some contacts will be more open to texting than others. You can use this method of communication when you have identified the contacts who are open to it. I have found that texting is a faster way to get a response, even if it's a simple acknowledgment, thumbs up or smiley emoji. Remember that texting can often lack a personal touch so be careful.

These are some examples of text messages you can send to your contact:

- Congratulations on closing the deal!
- What did you think of your presentation today?
-
- Simply check in to see how your project progresses.
-

Have you ever tried to get in touch?

Just wanted to say hello!

TIP...

Follow your social media contacts and follow them when they share positive news or a notable status update. It's the perfect time to send a text following up.

What's for Lunch?

Everyone loves a free lunch, but there is no such thing. This misconception can be changed by offering lunch to your contacts once per month, with no strings attached. There shouldn't be any strings attached. Then what's the agenda? Or as I like it to say, "What's for Lunch?" Answer: Use your network to help your contacts make connections and to assist each other with their business issues, challenges, and opportunities. This is how you help your contacts expand their networks and grow their businesses. This will be a very popular dish to serve. These lunches are a great way to get to know your contacts and learn more about how they fit in your network!

You will want to build relationships and extend your network beyond you and one contact. You can choose two to three business contacts, or invite people who would like to get together. Warning: This can be difficult and takes some finesse. Start with one person and then, during lunch, discover who they would prefer to meet. Invite that person to lunch next month. Voila! You now have two guests. This should continue to grow. You can limit the number of lunch attendees to four people. However, it is worth considering having more than one lunch each month. This event should be scheduled as a monthly one on your calendar. Make sure you schedule reminders for people to get on the list.

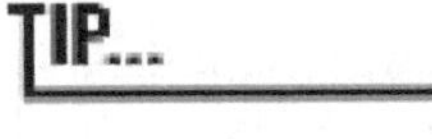

Jayson Gaignard has written Mastermind Dinners. This book is for people who are looking to build and sustain meaningful relationships. This book teaches you how to host dinners that create connections and allow you to use your network to solve other people's problems. Jason has made it easy and explained everything clearly.

Frosty Fridays

There's nothing better than treating yourself to a Wendy's Frosty T, especially on hot days or on not-so hot days. Frosties are delicious all year round. Part milkshake, part

This ice cream is unrivaled. Frosties have been a trademark of Wendy's for decades. You can also become famous through association. Treat your business contacts to Frosty Fridays and quickly make a name. Frosty Fridays can be a lot more enjoyable and less stressful than Taco Tuesdays. Why? Tacos are delicious, but they're too complicated to deliver.

Frosty Friday doesn't just revolve around the Frosty, it's also about showing appreciation to your contacts. Drop by your contact's workplace every Friday with a few Frosties. You'll find them enjoying Wendy's delicious treats. You'll find that you get more requests for Frosty Fridays as you go through your contacts.

You will give TGIF a new meaning. TGIF will be renamed TGIFF (Thank God It's Frosty Friday) because of your efforts!

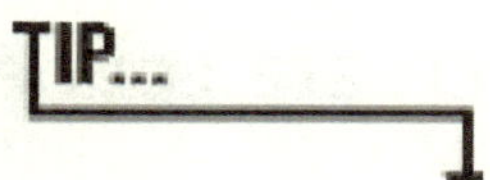

Keep the Frosties cool by keeping a cooler in your car. It'll be just like an ice cream truck but better. You'll love the hand-delivery of your treats to your contacts.

→

Biz Blogging

If you have a blog, please include a post that was inspired by someone and mention them. Many of your contacts are writers of blogs, articles or long-form social media posts. This information can be used to inspire blog posts. Then be

Include your contact information in the article, and link back to their site. They will also appreciate you sharing the article.

People have been asking me for inspiration for writing blogs and articles for years. There are many places to start: books you've read, success stories of clients, conversations at the office or frequently asked questions that you get while doing business. Your contacts are the best place to start!

Invite contacts who write articles or blog to become guest bloggers. It will be a great honor for your contacts to ask. Your site will get more traffic and you will both benefit. It's a win for everyone!

TIP...

If you have written a blog post that was inspired by someone, you should post it on Facebook, LinkedIn, or Twitter. This will increase exposure and drive traffic back to your blog. Send an email with an inspirational excerpt along with a link to your mailing list.

A Cure for the Monday Blues

There's nothing worse than Monday blues. You drag yourself to work and shuffle towards your office. It makes you wish that you were still at the backyard barbecue or ballgame with your friends. The Monday morning dread that creeps in often comes on Sunday night. We don't hate our jobs, but our weekends are filled with fun, friends and freedom, so it can be difficult to return to work.

You don't have it to be this way. It is possible to make things better for your contacts. You can't change Monday mornings, but you can surprise your contacts with freshly brewed coffee deliveries. The coffee surprise will make your contacts so happy that they can tackle everything. Your special touch is what made it possible.

How do you best accomplish this? You can hand deliver it yourself. If your contact is far away, this could prove difficult. GrubHub.com can help you get your coffee hot and delivered to your contact. This is the best way to get rid of Monday blues.

TIP...

Add some croissants, muffins, or scones to your coffee. It's just what the doctor ordered. You'll be loved even more if you add a dozen donuts to your coffee. But don't tell him about them, he might not be very happy with you.

Virtual Coffee

Do you want to brighten the day of your contact? You can send them a virtual cup of coffee by sending them an email to their favorite coffee shop. Don't just default to Starbucks, not everyone likes it. You can find out where your loved ones like to drink coffee and order the gift cards online. The delivery cost of a gift card will vary depending on the country from which it is sent.

Once you've given the gift of java, it's a perfect opportunity to follow up with your contact and schedule a virtual coffee with them. Get a date on the calendar to connect. Then start the conversation with: "How's your coffee?"

TIP...

Some companies allow you to send gift cards via iMessage. For example, Starbucks just requires you to enable mobile payments which works in conjunction with the Starbucks app. For other com-panies' step by step instructions, go to their websites.

Of Mice and Men

As the popular saying goes: the best-laid plans of mice and men sometimes go awry. This is from a poem by the Scottish poet Robert Burns, about a mouse that carefully builds a winter nest in a wheat field, only for it to be destroyed by a farmer. As with the hard-working mouse, things in business and in life don't always go as planned.

If one of your contacts is going through a rough patch—low sales, loss of a client, or their top performer left the company for another job—help them through it. Be present and available to listen—really listen—and remind them it won't always be like this. Sometimes all people need is for someone to reflect what they're feeling and to have faith in them when their faith in themselves is less than present.

Life is filled with ups and downs—it's quite the rollercoaster ride—and you don't always know the kind of day your contact is having. However, if you find out they are having a down day, reach out to them. Go out of your way to show your care and concern. That will make all the difference in the world, and it could turn their day around.

TIP...

When you discover your contact is having a rough time, it's a great time to send a handwritten note. There's nothing like a heartfelt card to convey that you're thinking about them.

Brain Hacking with Books

There's no easier or cheaper way to become an expert on a topic than by picking up a book that's packed with wisdom, practical advice, and tips.

Let's say your contact is struggling with some aspect of their business or is interested in a new line of business and needs an easily accessible solution. This is where business book recommendations come in handy. Don't just recommend a book; go one step further. Send your contact a book that will help them hone their products or services, and increase customer satisfaction and sales.

When speaking with contacts about their businesses, I'll mention books that have had a significant impact on my business life. I always have at least one copy of my favorite books ready to ship. If I see that a contact is interested, I'll personalize a note in the front of the book and send it off. Every time I send a book, I order another one from Amazon. The reason that this matters to your contact is due to the personalized note that you write in the book. To do that you need to ensure that the books are shipped to you first. Never order a book and ship it directly to your contact.

Some of my favorite business books include:

- *Never Eat Alone* by Keith Ferrazzi
- *E-Myth* by Michael Gerber
- *Profit First* by Mike Michalowicz
- *Never Lose A Customer Again* by Joey Coleman
- *Unthink* by Erik Wahl

Keep books in your Amazon cart where you can monitor price changes. If the price drops, buy several copies of your favorite book and stock up!

Hope You Can Come!

If your company has a customer appreciation night, invite your contact. If it's appropriate, also invite their significant other. Including your contact in your events, deepens your relationships. The effort to invite them won't go unnoticed, even if they cannot attend.

One summer I was invited to a customer appreciation night by the bank where I had my business account. The event was held at a modern art museum and included a band, an open bar, and a dinner with a seafood buffet. The event was absolutely amazing.

I had always been happy with my business bank and wouldn't have had a problem referring them, but the truth is I didn't really think about them much. If someone asked me who I used for business banking I would cite my bank's name, but if someone was considering taking out a loan or opening a business, I often didn't think to recommend my bank. The night of the event, I truly felt like a valued customer. Because of that, my bank made it to the top of my mind. When you invite your contacts to your special event, you will make a lasting impression.

TIP...

Pay special attention to which contacts you invite. If you invite too many, your time will be divided amongst all of them and as such your conversations will be diluted and remain at the surface level. Less is more in this case. I know this goes against the grain of trying to fill a room, but that goal is different from the goal of inviting a contact to deepen your relationship.

Play Matchmaker

One way you can make a splash is by playing matchmaker for your contacts. Tap into your extensive network of contacts to make meaningful connections that will enhance your contacts' businesses.

What's the best approach for doing this? Take time to ask your contacts about their ideal referrals. Identify your contacts' goals for their business and seek to understand how they define a good referral—someone who can help them in their business. Dig deeply into this.

I find that some contacts aren't clear about who is ideal for them. For example, a banker might say, anyone who runs a business; however, when you dig deeper, that isn't the case. While it's true that a banker can work with someone in another part of the country, it's not ideal for the banker or the customer. So, if you were helping the banker network with others, you would focus on contacts in the banker's local area.

Pay close attention to what your contact says about their ideal referral, and then ask follow-up questions, trying to identify exactly who would be a good contact for them. Once you do, identify people in your network and make an introduction—either virtually or in person.

TIP...

Establish a basic list of five to ten questions that you can ask your contact to dig deeper into how they define their ideal client. You may not use all of these each time, but you can start the conversation and delve into these questions when needed.

Giving Back

Caring comes in many forms and taking time to give back to causes that are important to your contacts will show them that you truly care. Does your contact support a specific charity or organization that you would? If they do, provide an item for a fundraiser, make a donation to their favorite organization, volunteer with your contact, or get the word out for a charity event they are organizing.

When it comes to giving back, it's important to give because you want to, and not because your contact gives to that charity. This is not about obligatory giving. If you are planning to give to your contacts' charities, determine if they align with your beliefs. If so, then give. If not, don't! You should give because you want to, not just because your contact does so.

TIP...

There's a new trend in which people celebrate their birthdays by fundraising for their favorite cause or charity on Facebook. Consider contributing to your contacts' selected causes for their birthdays. It's quick, easy, and it will make an impression.

Tricks of the Trade

You typically know more about your products or services than your contacts do. Share a tip or trick that will make their life easier, regardless of whether they are using your products or services. For example, when I owned my website agency, getting content from clients was a huge challenge. We found that very few people were aware of transcription services that existed and all the different options that were available. These services allow for people to record audio and have it transcribed into the written word. Creating content was stressful for clients and these services made creating content less stressful, so we shared them with both clients and contacts. Sharing these ideas, suggestions and tips with your contacts can assist them in improving and streamlining their business processes and lives. They will be grateful for your expertise and your generosity in sharing what you know.

TIP...

Be sure to track in your CRM or a Spreadsheet what you are sending to your contacts so that you don't send them duplicate tips or suggestions.

What's in a Name?

What's in a name? Well, everything. Dale Carnegie said, "A person's name is to him or her the sweetest and most important sound in any language."

Consider this: how does it feel when someone gets your name wrong? It comes across as if that person doesn't care enough to get it right. How about when someone surprises you by knowing your name when you don't even know theirs? You're delighted and a little embarrassed that you couldn't return the favor.

When interacting with a contact, make sure to use their name. When should you do this? Several times during each interaction. Let's say your contact's name is Connie. When greeting her, smile, shake her hand, and say, "Nice to see you again, Connie." When leaving, say, "Thank you for meeting with me today, Connie. I really appreciate it." Begin every email with, *Hi Connie*, and end with, *thank you, Connie*.

Now, make sure you don't overdo this. If you overuse your contact's name, as in inserting it in every other sentence, it can sound insincere. You don't want to come across like the bad stereotype of a used car salesperson. So, if this is new for you, start slowly and use your contact's name a few times during your exchange. Working a contact's name into a conversation may seem awkward at first, but you will adjust and see the benefits of the relationship grow.

When communicating by email, spend a little extra time ensuring that you spell your contact's name correctly. It will be well worth it. You can usually find their name in their email address or signature.

TIP...

If you are unsure how to pronounce a contact's name, there is no shame in asking them how to pronounce it. It is better to ask than to mispronounce or avoid using it.

Pause and Listen

Imagine this: your contact calls you and they are really hyped up, but you are completely swamped. Your contact is talking a mile a minute about an aerospace stock that they invested in years ago and they are finally seeing a return. They are delving into specific details of the aerospace industry, as well as the history.

Is this something that you want to listen to right now? No! Is this something you are interested in? No! Are you going to give your contact your undivided attention? Yes! Why? Because you care about your contact and you know that listening is one of the key components of your personal care package. As you turn your attention to the conversation, you may soon develop an interest in aerospace, at least as it pertains to this conversation. Your contact will appreciate your undivided attention. And you never know —you could decide to invest in the aerospace stock and it could become your best investment ever!

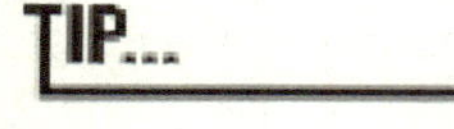

Most of us think we're skilled at multitasking, but the truth is: none of us are. So when your contact calls and talks about a subject that's not particularly interesting to you, turn away from your digital devices and truly listen. if you're looking at your emails or text messages, you won't be fully present and it will be a missed opportunity to connect with your contact.

Five Star Review

With social media reigning supreme in most industries, few things are more valuable for driving sales than rave reviews. And, on the contrary, a few scathing reviews can destroy a business. Glowing reviews are like gold in this era of social media domination and can really solidify trust for those looking for new services.

Consider taking 10 minutes out of your day to write a review for your contact on social media. There are lots of ways to review contacts and their businesses. A simple shout-out while tagging your contact on Facebook, Instagram, or Twitter will let your friends and followers know that your contact's business is trustworthy. For increased impact consider a formal review on a notable review site. You'll have to identify the site that reviews your contact's industry. For example, if your contact is in the travel industry, use websites like TripAdvisor or Yelp. Or if they are in the restaurant business, Open Table, Zagat, or Zomato are popular sites.

Becoming a raving fan is about sharing your experience as a customer, partner, or colleague. If you've never had a transaction then you can talk about the merits of your contact's integrity as a businessperson.

TIP...

To write a review, take a quick peek at the other reviews and make sure yours doesn't simply mimic existing reviews. Write something new that showcases your contact's business in an attention-grabbing way. Draft a review, edit it, and then post it for the world to see.

Game Time!

Imagine receiving a call from a contact inviting you to see your favorite sports team play. How awesome would you feel? Even if you can't attend, knowing that someone is thinking about you would make you feel great.

Consider inviting your contacts to a game to get caught up in the thrill of victory and the agony of defeat. Sporting events are shared experiences that go deeper than most. When you attend a game with someone who shares the love of the game and the love of the team, the camaraderie is unparalleled.

In 2018, I took one of my contacts to the AFC Championship game in Foxboro, Massachusetts. The New England Patriots hosted the Jacksonville Jaguars. We had a great time connecting on a personal level, sharing the game together, and experiencing yet another amazing come-from-behind win by Tom Brady. I've had similar experiences at hockey, golf, basketball, and badminton. Okay, maybe not badminton. But every game experience has been memorable and helped to cement my relationships with my contacts.

TIP...

Try to steer clear of business talk during game day. Just be there for the game, to connect, build a deeper relationship, and to have fun!

Fore!

Yes, we're talking golf here. And while it might sound like a cliché', golf will never go out of fashion when it comes to bringing people together and garnering good favor. True, you don't want to invite a contact on a golf outing if they don't play – no better way to embarrass someone or bore them silly – but for those of us who do play, it's a great way to create a relaxed atmosphere that may or may not lead to business-related conversation. Even if it doesn't, the goodwill you've established will come back to you in spades.

I am always receiving notifications about golf tournaments in my area, because I've made a point of joining organizations that use golf for fundraising purposes. I automatically sign up for a foursome and intentionally invite three of my best contacts, people whom I know like golf. The beauty of it is, something as simple as 18 holes of golf establishes deeper connections that are both professional and personal. A no-brainer.

The reason this works is that you've taken the time to reach out to people who know you and your business, but you've taken the business out of it. You're playing golf with people you like and you're footing the bill. People remember that. Don't think that won't come back to you when someone needs your services. If your contacts end up helping each other, even better.

TIP...

Join organizations that organize golf tournaments for fundraising purposes, such as Make-A-Wish, Rotary International, your industry association and your local chamber of commerce.

Red Carpet Events

Who doesn't love to celebrate someone on the red carpet? Perhaps your contact is being honored at an industry event, having an open house, or a ribbon-cutting ceremony. Or maybe your contact is giving a keynote speech or offering a workshop. Especially if your contact is local, make sure you are there. You don't have to attend every event, but you should attempt to get to a few of them. This will make a huge impact. Your contact will be thrilled you took the time to attend their event. In fact, they will never forget it. Making the effort to honor them will make a lasting impression. Not only that, you'll learn more about them, their industry, and it will deepen and strengthen your relationship.

Consider attending a contact's out-of-town event. If you are planning an upcoming business trip, do some research on your contacts' events, show up, and surprise them! They will be touched and delighted and you will have a contact for life.

TIP...

To stay on top of your contacts' special events, research their upcoming events and create a contact spreadsheet. Add the event information from the spreadsheet to your calendar.

The Grand Tour

When you are at your contact's place of business, ask for a tour, especially if it is a factory or warehouse. It's very likely you will learn something new about your contact, as well as their business and industry. Your contact will be flattered by your interest in their business. If a tour isn't available at the time, but you are offered one in the future, don't hesitate to get it on the calendar.

Whenever I am offered a tour, I enthusiastically accept the invitation. It's such a great learning experience for me and it gives me plenty of opportunities to ask questions and engage with my contact, which creates more understanding. The insight gained allows me to more effectively help my contact in the future.

TIP...

This is a great opportunity, if permitted, to shoot videos for future sharing on social media. Make sure to ask your contact for permission, as some facilities may forbid photography of any kind due to the sensitive nature of the business or industry.

Pick Up the Tab

Attending networking events is a very effective way to grow your contact base, meet great people, and establish deeper more meaningful connections. While it can be effective to pick up the drink tab for one or more contacts, it's far more effective to pick up the registration tab for your contact to attend the event .

When you decide to attend an event, reach out to a few contacts and invite them along. Attending networking events is far less daunting for some people when they know that there will be a friendly face in the crowd as well.

This can make the event far more effective for you and for them.

TIP...

When one of your contacts accepts your invitation and attends the event, make a point to introduce them to others that you know. Additionally, as you meet new people throughout the event, circle back and introduce your contact to them as well.

Extend an Offer

The second pillar of your personal care package is listening. If you hear that your contact is going on a trip, volunteer to drive them to the airport.

You will save them money, have time to reconnect on a personal level, and they will be very grateful for your assistance.

You might see on Facebook that they are looking for a dog sitter for the weekend, and you like dogs. Call them and volunteer to dog sit.

Maybe your contact is looking for someone to mow their lawn. If you have a teenager, send them over.

There are so many ways you can extend an offer and lend a hand, it's up to your imagination and your ability to listen to what is going on around you with your contacts.

TIP...

When offering to lend a hand, don't accept any money in exchange for your time or work. If you send over your child to mow their lawn, don't let them accept money. Instead you pay them for their time and work.

Going Once...
Going Twice...
Gone!

Many businesses participate in local charity auctions, and sometimes they are very involved. Consider this as a great avenue to help your contact.

Businesses get involved in charity auctions in many different ways. Sometimes they are organizing the event, other times they volunteer to help during the event, and then of course there are companies that are donating an auction item. Regardless of their level of involvement, you can find ways to participate with them and help their auction be a sweet success.

Are there items or services that you can donate from your business that they could in turn auction off? If your business is not well suited for auction donations, buy an item from another contact and donate that item to the auction. You'll be helping two contacts in this situation.

TIP...

To start the auction conversation, simply share with your contact a story about a previous auction you participated in, then ask if they have ever done similar events. You'll find out really quick if they are involved with any charity auctions!

Getting Started

In my experience, after introducing the concept of caring to audiences and clients, they get excited and rush out and buy Thank You Cards in bulk! A word of caution. Slow and steady wins this race.

My suggestion is that you start with six contacts and get to know them better. Start working on growing deeper connections with them. Understand who they are, what their needs are and look to give them referrals. Focus on these six contacts for the first 90 days.

Each month thereafter, consider adding one additional contact each month until you reach 12. Once you have your core 12 contacts, continue building your relationships with them for at least one full year without adding others into the mix.

This doesn't mean you ignore others, but it does mean you keep your focus on the 12.

I also suggest that the 12 key contacts be people you already have a relationship with. Ideally, they are someone that has potential to refer business. This won't always be the case, and there are exceptions to every rule, but I have found this to be the most successful way to jumpstart a word of mouth referral system.

Let it be known that not everyone you want to establish a relationship is interested in that. I have worked to grow relationships with people only to realize over time that they just aren't a relationship person. At some point, you need to move on. I'm not saying you shouldn't care any longer, I'm just saying that you shouldn't put the same amount of effort into building a stronger relationship with that contact.

So how do you know? They simply don't respond. This isn't determined by whether or not they give you referrals. It's determined by the fact that they engage. They reply. They call you back. If they are not engaging with you at all over a long period of time, that's when you say to yourself "It's not me, it's you"

Final Thought

Over the course of building your personal CarePackage, you will see contacts come and go. That is normal. Embrace the process. There will be change within your contacts and understand that these changes are for the better. You'll be learning how to interact with your contacts as you go along, and your skills will grow. You'll get better at connecting, and you will start to see relationships in ways that you may have never seen them before.

This process for me started many years ago. It was slow in the beginning. I didn't reach out as much. I didn't get out of my comfort zone and give more. But now, I give all the time. I find ways to overdeliver as much as I feasibly can, while at the same time really understanding who I am talking to by listening to them and researching what they are all about. Sometimes, I even surprise myself with surprises for others! But at the end of the day, this isn't about me, this is about my contacts. Everything I do is in service of them, and I ensure I am driven by the fourth pillar in my personal CarePackage, Non-Self-Serving acts.

www.ingramcontent.com/pod-product-compliance
Lightning Source LLC
LaVergne TN
LVHW090136160826
845673LV00017B/2489

* 9 7 9 8 7 7 5 7 7 8 6 3 7 *